A Woman's Guide to

Balancing Career and Family:

Solutions for Your Job, Your Family and Yourself

Edited by National Press Publications

NATIONAL PRESS PUBLICATIONS

A Division of Rockhurst University Continuing Education Center, Inc.
6901 West 63rd Street • P.O. Box 2949 • Shawnee Mission, Kansas 66201-1349
1-800-258-7248 • 1-913-432-7757

National Press Publications endorses gender equality and general respect. As this book is geared toward women, "she" is used. There are examples and points of view that exemplify varying generalizations. The many studies cited are derived from such sources as the U.S. Census, Center for Creative Leadership, American Society of Training and Development and university reports. Not intended to be sexist or biased, the copy challenges beliefs.

A Woman's Guide to Balancing Career and Family: Solutions for Your Job, Your Family and Yourself

Published by National Press Publications, Inc.
Copyright 2001 National Press Publications, Inc.
A Division of Rockhurst University Continuing Education Center, Inc.

Printed in the United States of America

 2 3 4 5 6 7 8 9 10

ISBN 1-55852-271-9

Table of Contents

INTRODUCTION

This book is here to help you cope with the effects of stress and burnout by:

- Giving practical tips on household chores.

- Providing pointers for finding good child-care or elderly care providers and ways to protect your loved ones.

- Showing how to get the assistance you need from your place of work.

- Showing how to train and change attitudes of family members to make them part of the solution instead of adding to the problem.

- Pointing out how to transfer office skills to home and vice versa for effective life balance.

- Providing suggestions for finding time for your partner, your children, elderly dependents, your friends, extended family and special interests and still making time to nurture yourself.

- Suggesting how to prioritize and organize better to get more done.

- Passing on hints and experiences of real working women.

- Providing information on the latest research, facts and figures that let you know you are not alone.

- Giving special encouragement for single and "solo" women.

- Giving information for sandwich-generation women who are looking after elders.

- Showing places to go to get more help.

- Creating a life filled with personal interests.

- Learning how to enjoy being with "you."

> *"Almost two-thirds of employees are responsible for caring for a child, an aging relative or both. The need to find a reasonable balance is overwhelming for a huge number of people."*
>
> — Ann Douglas

1 CAREER, FAMILY, SELF

A realistic life goal, or an invitation to the three-ring circus, starring Superwoman as Ringmaster Mom?

Welcome to the "Greatest Show on Earth"

Three rings full of action that spill in a nonstop life and leave you breathless. Directing it all: Ringmaster Mom, the director and star of every act. From taming dust bunnies and the boss to juggling deadlines and doctors' appointments, she plunges into the laundry, scoots kids off to school, swings by the store, lassoes the new account, and clowns around with friends in a death-defying attempt to keep everyone happy.

The amazing Ringmaster Mom! Who but Superwoman could even try to take on this role? One minute she's motivating the team; the next, she's organizing the PTA bake sale. A quick-change artist without equal, she moves from power suit to jogging suit in a blink of an eye.

How Does She Do It — and Why?

The fact is that Superwoman, June Cleaver and the Little Red Hen are fictional characters. They do not exist now, or ever.

We can now say with truth that, once upon a time, way back in the last century, for a few brief years, and for no good reason, some people thought that they could be a superwoman if they tried hard enough. They succeeded only in beating themselves (and a subsequent generation of women) over the heads with the misguided notion that they could do it.

In this new century, a more enlightened attitude is needed. It's time for those women, who because of necessity or choice work outside their homes, to find a happier balance for living. It's time to settle for a kinder, gentler lifestyle, geared to more reasonable attitudes and expectations of and by women.

> *"If at first you don't succeed, you're running about average."*
>
> — Anonymous

Superwoman was expected to have a wonderfully fulfilling career; two perfect children; an adoring, spoiled-rotten spouse; and a circle of charming, supportive friends. She gave selflessly to worthy civic causes, took an intelligent interest in politics and world events, cheered all the home-team games and played excellent tennis. Dressed to perfection, she had her hair and nails done weekly and never gained a pound. Her skirt never bagged, her hose never ran, her mascara never smudged. From gleaming, uncluttered counters to lush, weed-free lawns, her home reflected the ordered serenity of her exquisite self. How many women today still secretly long for this unattainable, idealized life as if it were somehow possible?

Even if your job is dull and poorly paid, your children get barely average marks in school, and your spouse is as tired and dissatisfied as you are, do you still stubbornly uphold the myth that if you only work harder you can make the dream come true?

Whining friends, a demanding extended family, and impositions from the organizations you wish you hadn't joined may be the reality, but deep down you know you could fix it if you could only find the magic words. There just has to be a simple trick to looking like a model in your chain-store bargain clothes and $2 lipstick. The house and garden will look great next year, just as soon as you get organized. You can do it all — if you only try.

Wherever the Superwoman Myth sprang from, and however removed it has become from reality today, the fact remains it is a myth. Superwoman is fiction and you believe in her at your peril.

Working Women

The majority of mothers are now employed outside the home. In fact, more than 60 percent of all women in the United States are working outside the home either full- or part-time and comprise approximately 50 percent of the total work force.

Service jobs account now for more than two-thirds of all jobs, and women are engaged in a majority of these positions. Women tend to be involved chiefly in clerical, service, professional/specialty, sales and middle-management positions. Their greatest numbers are to be found in health care where they comprise over three-fourths of workers in all sectors. Increasing numbers of women are entering traditionally male fields such as financial services, trades, transportation and construction.

Even if women truly wanted to return to a 1950s-style family structure, it is doubtful that the economic health of the nation could sustain such a move. It is still less likely that the average family could manage without Mom's paycheck. Even if we ignore the large segment of the population where the sole family support is borne by the mother, statistics indicate that a significant number of all two-parent families would fall below the poverty line if they relied on only one salary for support. This helps to explain why so many single-parent families are struggling financially.

It is also true that the average North American family has a much higher expectation of owning material goods that were once considered luxuries available to only the privileged few. Items such as computers, VCRs, convection ovens, sports-utility vehicles, electronic games and digital cameras, etc. are readily available and widely advertised. Many people cannot imagine life without two or more cars, multiple television sets, mountain bikes for everyone, and a variety of sports and exercise equipment. A return to a simpler lifestyle is not an option that many Americans might embrace.

At the same time that the desire for more material possessions has grown, the real earnings of many people, especially of younger men, have actually decreased. Fewer benefits, downsizing and the need to return to college, trade school or university to retrain for new career options are facts of life. These circumstances have decreased the ability of a single breadwinner to earn enough to maintain a family — especially one with the high material expectations that are "normal" for today. Women who once worked from choice are finding themselves compelled to remain in the work force in ways that have not been experienced since they were pushed into filling men's jobs on the home front during World War II.

Not too long ago, whether women did or did not, perception was that very few worked outside the home. Today, these women are acknowledged because the income from work outside the home is vital to maintaining their family.

Another interesting change has happened in our society. It is one that really changes the way family life has been traditionally perceived. While the earning power of young men has declined, that of younger women has increased. In some two-parent families, the woman's earnings are higher than the man's. More and more couples are considering the option, once so strange as to be unthinkable, of having the father stay home with the children while the mother, the one with the larger paycheck, goes out to work.

Options about working do still exist for some women. There are just as many of the old reasons for and against employment outside the home as there ever were. But now, several new items for consideration have been added to the problem, and some of the old arguments have lost their validity for many families.

Payoffs and Sacrifices

The basic pros and cons remain the same. The extra income is the biggest factor when deciding to work, with career mapping and personal satisfaction as additional incentives for many women. The negative side remains one largely dominated by feelings of guilt, stress and too much to do in too little time. Many women experience the effects of all these arguments at the same time. They may feel trapped and powerless by living in an unresolved state where they both need and want to work while needing and wanting (at the same time) to stay home and look after their families.

Younger children need to have support to ensure that they make the trip safely. It may mean extra juggling of your time to ensure that they get the care they need, but it is worthwhile for your own peace of mind as well as their well-being.

Couples can often arrange things so that one or the other's work schedule allows them to cover both ends of the day. Grandparents or stay-at-home friends and neighbors might also be willing to help. Older children are also a good resource for getting small children to and from school. Many schools make a conscious effort to arrange school-bus schedules so that older children are available to help smaller children get home safely.

Children need a safe place to call or go to if they feel threatened in any way while going to and from school. Block-parent programs are popular in many neighborhoods, and teaching your children to look for the signs or to get to know a few of the families on their route is a good idea.

Children need to be taught "street smarts." This includes road safety as well as looking out for scary strangers. Most schools now also teach children to be careful of hazards of all kinds.

Teach your child how to avoid letting strangers know that he is alone, or that you will not be home to greet him when he gets there.

Neighbors are usually the best emergency help there is for your child. Having a good relationship with your neighbors, knowing that they will shelter your child in a crisis, is an excellent security resource for children of all ages. Make sure that your neighbor has a current work number for you and your husband, and do not overuse this resource by asking them to baby-sit or take on too much responsibility for your children. There are parents who will say that they'll be fine putting in a couple of hours of overtime because their kid is playing at the neighbor's, and they'll be sure to give him some supper if he hangs around long enough! This is not fair to your child or your neighbor. Save your emergency backup for when you really need it and keep on good terms with your neighbor.

Children should be told to stick to a consistent route to and from school and not go wandering off alone. It is usually better if children walk with friends and stick together rather than go alone. Those who cycle must know safety rules and follow them rigorously.

If the child stops at a friend's house or has to stay later than usual at school, he must be taught to call you immediately.

Allowing children to bring friends home when you aren't there isn't a good idea. Children get into trouble very easily when there are two or three of them unsupervised in the house.

If it's nice weather, then children are often happy to play outside in the yard, walk their dog, or play with neighbor children until you get home.

If your rule is for the child to come home and do homework, then that is what should happen. Allowing children to break rules when they are home alone undermines their security and your peace of mind.

"Test your child's street savvy by conducting role-playing sessions. Turn it into a game of 'What if?' For example, ask the child what he would do if someone came along in a car as he was walking from school and said he was from his dad's office, that his dad had been hurt, and that they had come to take him to see his dad in the hospital. Let the child respond and then work together on ways to get him out of the situation safely."

— Marion Thomas, National Press Publications

Sexual Abuse

Fears that your child may be left in the care of someone who will abuse the trust that has been given are very real. Most parents have these fears. The high rates of child sexual abuse show such fears to be well-founded in fact. Figures suggesting that one-fourth of girls and about half that number of boys will suffer some inappropriate sexual contact before the age of 18 are grounds for concern.

The fact is that most sexual abuse is from people the child knows well. Family members make up the majority of offenders.

There is very little evidence that suggests a higher risk for children of working parents, however. In fact, having a child in a well-chosen day-care facility may be an excellent protection against abuse.

Talking to children before abuse happens will also be a good way to prevent it from happening at all. Teach children how to respond to approaches from strangers and any behavior from anyone, even someone they know well, that make them uneasy.

Letting your child know that he can say anything to you without making you angry is a good first step. Listening to children and taking their fears, hints, hypothetical statements and questions seriously will help them keep important lines of communication open.

The way your child acts might lead you to suspect abuse has happened, even if nothing has been said.

Behavioral Indicators of Child Sexual Abuse

- Sudden changes in behavior

- Sexual behavior with other children

- Refusal to undress in front of you or the doctor

- Reluctance to go to certain locations

- Comments about sexual involvement, touching or kissing with adults

- Poor peer relationships

- Low self-esteem

Physical Indicators of Child Sexual Abuse

- Sexually transmitted disease

- Pain or itching in the genital area

- Torn, stained or bloody clothing, especially underclothes

Sexual abuse of children is a criminal offense and must be reported to police. Procedures for dealing with abused children are much better directed than in the past. Your child may need medical attention or counseling. Abused children need lots of strong parental support and extra attention to overcome their trauma. It may become necessary for a parent to stay home for a while to handle the special needs of this child.

There is no way to guarantee your child's safety — even when you are with him. Providing the safest environment possible is the best you can do.

Your primary role is to take as many precautions as reasonably possible and train your child to take care of himself. Children are remarkably resourceful. Stories of 2-year-olds dialing 911 to get help for an unconscious mother or of 4-year-olds dragging baby brothers out of house fires are not that uncommon.

Share stories like these with your child. Talking up the positive results of knowing how to handle problems rather than transferring your fears and worries to your children will help them cope with confidence when things go wrong.

Twelve Tips for Getting Off on the Right Foot

Start day care on a positive note that will help your child enjoy the experience.

1. Don't cry till you get back outside. Your little ones will cry if you do — even if they don't understand why. Put on a happy face and keep your fears and worries well hidden.

2. Tell them you love them and will be back soon to get them and take them home again.

3. Explain day care carefully to children who are old enough to understand. Make it into a story with your child as the star.

4. Don't sneak out when the upset child isn't looking, or you might set up a fear of being abandoned.

5. Try to have time to stay to see your child established in an activity before you leave.

6. Handing a younger child into the caregiver's arms rather than allowing him to be taken from you seems to be easier on a child somehow.

7. Arrange to stay for part of the day or pick him up early. Staying and playing until the usual time to leave will let your child know that you are involved in his day and like him being where he is.

8. Don't be surprised if your child cries when you come to pick him up. Emotions for children are most fully expressed in the company of those they love most. Some children stoically refuse to let go all day but feel able to let it all hang out with Mom.

Reflections

Waiting for your partner to notice the dirt and do something about it, or realize you are annoyed that he hasn't and didn't is unrealistic to say the least. Never forget that the same person who tells you not to nag will also tell you to ask if you want something.

- Draw up a list and agree who does what — up-front.

- Avoid adding on chores you forgot afterwards. It's better to renegotiate next year than try to stick in extras midseason.

- Hang up the list where he can see it so you don't have to remind him (nag) each week to do what he agreed to.

- Help him sometimes if he's really pushed.

- Validate and encourage his efforts.

- Don't be too picky about the results.

- Don't carp if he has different ways of working than you do. So what if he does the laundry differently? As long as he's doing it and you aren't, do you really care how it's done? If you answered "yes," then you've just found the reason for your stress.

Team dynamics in the workplace suggest that teams made up of people with diverse skills are more productive than those of members with similar skills. Try viewing diversity of approach to household tasks as a plus.

Divide tasks according to strengths as well as personal preferences. Be flexible and open to changes of task distribution from time to time.

If workloads change, or if one partner goes back to school or has to be away on business trips, the ability to be flexible must exist. If another baby comes along, then everything will be different.

There is plenty of evidence out there to suggest that the ways couples divide tasks undergo profound changes over time.
Studies of aging show that many couples experience a role reversal in later life. Women who enter or go back into the work force after their children have grown up are seen to become much more career oriented. People, especially those taking early retirement, find they now enjoy household tasks. They may begin cooking or redecorating, pursuing activities they never tried when younger. This profound change affects many couples and may explain why quite a large number of women who choose a late career do very well in the workplace and decide to stay at work even though their partners are no longer working outside the home at all.

Child Care

There are very few fathers in the U.S. today who have never gotten up to help with their children in the night, or who cannot change diapers. The notion that men are not "supposed" to do these tasks seems alien to us today, but those attitudes were quite normal 50 or 60 years ago.

Today's dads enjoy interacting with their children. They may worry that they are not as closely bonded to their children as the mother. They are more concerned that they are not spending as much time as they should with their children.

Changes in custody laws reflect the desire felt by many men after divorce to keep close contact with their children.

Encouraging men to participate fully in every stage of a child's life is a way to keep men playing a meaningful role in caring for children. Fathering is important to American men. Having poor male models can be a cause of family violence and marriage breakdown. Many religious authorities stress the importance of excellence in fathering as a main contributor to stability, not just in families but also the community at large.

Men are becoming increasingly aware of the need to find a better balance between the demands made on their time by their jobs and the needs of their families.

You Can Help

Women can play an important part in giving their husbands time to be alone with the children. They need to teach child-care skills if their husbands seem diffident or unsure. Many women learn child-raising skills unconsciously from family members, while men still tend to be excluded from this process.

Both men and women are generally older now when starting out in the process of raising their own families. On average, in the latter part of the 20th century, adults started having children when they were in their late 20s or early 30s. Many people, especially those with post-secondary education or careers, will be even older — late 30s and early 40s are not unusual for this group.

Younger people tend to be somewhat more confident when it comes to trying new tasks, like raising children. They are less intimidated by fears of failure. Older parents tend to be more cautious and more likely to turn to traditional mores for guidance. Younger fathers are therefore less constrained about child care than older ones.

If your partner is older, he may need more encouragement to be an active, confident dad.

Many experts once thought that labor-saving devices and modern inventions would bring in an age of extended leisure and lots of spare time. This has not proved to be the case.

Which of the following "myths" have been used against you?

Myth — Frozen foods will mean no more wasting time in the kitchen.

Fact — Prepared foods are pricey, they may contain a lot of fat, preservatives and salt.

Balanced View

Convenience foods are useful in emergencies, but there are plenty of quick and easy-to-make foods, like stir-fry or pasta, that cost less and cook quicker than frozen meals.

Myth — Modern homes are easier to clean.

Fact — Average family homes are larger today than ever before. Ease of cleaning depends on personal decorating style and individual standards of hygiene.

Balanced View

You can make cleaning easier by your choice of furnishings and appliances. Matte paint and light-colored kitchen and bathroom surfaces show dust and fingerprints less. Only give the weekly cleaning job to rooms that are actually in use. Save cleaning spare rooms until you need to use them. Stain-resistant fabrics and clothing that don't need ironing will also cut down on chores.

Reflections

Myth — Modern gadgets cut down on time spent on household tasks.

Fact — This is true to a degree, but, in the past, extended families and servants shared the load of work done at home. Washing was often sent out. Gardeners and delivery boys helped make some chores much easier.

Balanced View

Too many gadgets simply add to clutter, especially in the kitchen. Keep only the things that you really use. For example, it's probably easier for most people to buy yogurt than have a yogurt maker sitting on the counter.

Myth — Power tools and machines make yard work a breeze.

Fact — Yards are bigger too. Gardening is popular now, and many more people enjoy it as a hobby. Machinery helps but also costs a lot, breaks down and needs maintenance.

Balanced View

In the past, yard work was seen as something done by the men of the family. Today, all the family can get involved, but mostly it's the men who get to use those neat power tools and equipment. Until recently, tools were large, heavy and cumbersome. It is at last getting easier to find tools that are suitable for women and teens to use. Large hardware chains are getting better at catering to women customers. Helping out in the yard and doing maintenance jobs may be ways of Dad doing more housework.

Reflections

- Avoid perfectionism.

- Validate the efforts of others.

- Consider their own needs to be on a par with the needs of others.

Go back over the list and check off the characteristics that you feel you share. Recognizing the strengths you already have is a good way to start building up those areas where you need more coping skills. Coping skills are a lot like physical abilities or business smarts; you can develop them and make them work better.

Susan Bixler and Lisa Scherrer, in their book *Take Action,* describe how some people have a harder time coping with stress because they wake up already feeling stressed. Unless they can find ways to lower their stress levels before leaving the house, they will blow their stacks long before reaching work. Perhaps this explains why we hear so much about road rage these days?

Try thinking about your ability to cope with frustrations and snags as like the shielding forcefield around the spaceship in a sci-fi movie. Attack weakens the shields, leaving the vessel vulnerable to enemy lasers. You need to find ways of strengthening your stress-shields to withstand the daily onslaught.

- Get a book, video- or audiotape to help you build some of the coping skills you need to brace up your stress-shield.

- Have fun.

- Practice relaxation techniques.

- Get over the need to reach impossible standards set for you by others.

- Build a support system of friends and family that you can count on for help in a crisis.

- Plan for possible problems like sudden loss of regular child care.

- Take five-minute vacations.

- Have dreams and long-term goals to help you get through the tough times.

- Top off your reserves by nurturing yourself, taking time for you.

Small Signs That Stress Levels Are Getting Too High

- Impatience

- Irritability

- Snapping at kids and husband when they goof up

- Testiness with fellow workers

- Carping about the boss

- Overindulging in things like coffee, cigarettes, alcohol and food

- Worry that keeps you awake at night

- Inability to concentrate or relax

- Forgetfulness

- Sleeping in

- Lateness and missed appointments

- Losing articles more often than usual

- Feeling weepy

- Losing your sense of humor

Listen when your partner or a friend or colleague recognizes these signs early. Acting on your stress-related problems before they get overwhelming is vital. As with any medical condition, early detection makes for an easier cure.

Serious Symptoms of Major Stress

- Headaches/migraine

- Heart problems

- Stomach disorders — ulcers or colitis

- High blood pressure

- Some kinds of arthritic problems

- Lowered resistance to viral infections

- Insomnia

- Muscular cramps and tension — neck and back problems

- Asthmatic reactions

- Depression

- Skin rashes or other allergic reactions

- Disorientation

- Withdrawal

- Obsessive-compulsive behavior

Many doctors believe that stress contributes to poor recovery of cancer patients, erratic blood-sugar levels in diabetics, and psychosomatic ailments.

A mother's stress is passed on to her unborn children in the womb as well as family members in general. Children with mental or physical problems may well be reacting to parental stress, which increases their own stress level.

Fertility levels and impotence are closely aligned to stress.

Stress is a major cause of accidents, especially accidents at work.

A study by the Occupational Safety and Health Administration (OSHA) surveyed more than 3,000 women. Sixty-one percent felt that they experienced high levels of stress. Not all stress is "in our heads." Musculoskeletal problems from repetitive stress account for hundreds of thousands of lost production days each year. Both men and women suffer back pain as a result of work-related stress. As women move into nontraditional jobs, some physical problems are changing. Jobs in the health-care industry have always involved both mental and physical injury. Back problems, accidental needle jabs, and violent patients are just a few of the stressful facts of life for medical workers.

Working can be hard on your health. Chemicals and radiation are a major source of workplace health hazards. Violence in the workplace, accidents and even workplace murder are growing problems. Trying to stay safe at work and while travelling to and from the workplace may add to your daily stress levels.

Experts agree that high stress levels increase your likelihood of having an accident, at home or in the workplace or while travelling. Stress causes you to lose concentration and act hurriedly — a deadly combination if you have to handle potentially dangerous equipment or drive a car.

It may also leave you vulnerable to violence if you're not paying attention to your surroundings, unaware of making mistakes that upset others, or not recognizing danger signs from people around you.

Self-Inflicted Stress

Allowing yourself to get behind in the morning, because you hit the snooze button or were trying to squeeze in just one more chore before going to the bus stop, is just asking for trouble. You'll remember the way you snapped at the children and missed the bus much longer than the extra 10 minutes of sleep.

If you constantly undermine yourself by causing yourself this kind of stress, start asking why. Do you hate your job so much that you can't bear to get there in the morning? Are you getting enough sleep?

Be honest with yourself and root out the reason for undermining yourself in this destructive way. You can control self-inflicted stress if you try.

Outside Stress

Stress that is outside your control is harder to handle.

> *"What's the difference between a stumbling block and a stepping-stone? It's all in the way you approach it."*
>
> — James Brady, President Reagan's Press Secretary, paralyzed after being shot in the head during an assassination attempt on the president

You may not be able to control the stressful situation, but you can learn how to control your reaction to it so that the stress does not overwhelm you.

Manage external stress better by:

1. Identifying the source.

   - Where is your stress coming from?

   - What can you do, if anything, to help you cope better?

   - Do you need to be more assertive about your needs?

   - Should you improve a relationship with a difficult co-worker?

   - Do you need to talk with your team leader?

   - Knowledge is power. Find out what you can about the problem so that you understand the situation thoroughly. Stressful reactions to people and events sometimes fade when we understand them better.

- Remind yourself of your skills and accomplishments?
- Reach out to others?
- Play?
- Do spontaneous things, just for the fun of it?
- Go on dates with your husband?
- Hang out with friends?
- Learn from your children?

e. Do you take care of your spiritual health?

> *"Grant me the serenity to accept the things I cannot change,*
> *courage to change the things I can,*
> *and wisdom to know the difference."*
>
> — Serenity Prayer

- Recognize that you have a spiritual component and look for ways to fulfill it?
- Attend religious services?
- Teach your children about their religious heritage?
- Share life experiences with family elders?
- Connect your children to their family history and cultural roots?
- Help your children understand your beliefs about life questions such as death, birth, human relationships and the structure of society?
- Try to be more understanding of the religious beliefs of others?
- Look for ways to build up the self-esteem and well-being of others?
- Do random acts of kindness?
- Reach out to others?
- Empathize with and support others when they have special needs?

Reflections

"No one else in this world can be you or live your life. Every moment of the day, if you are simply BEING, you are moving in the right direction. When you concentrate on BEING instead of doing or having, you will discover that you are living in excellence."

— Patricia Wilson, *Living in Excellence*

11 WORKING WITHOUT A NET

The special concerns of single mothers

There is no doubt that there are special challenges facing single-parent families in America today. Coping with growing children without support is very difficult, and many thousands of women are attempting to do just that task. In effect, these women try to fill the role of both parents. They may of necessity work full time and bear sole responsibility for maintaining home and family, also.

- Of the 70.9 million-plus families in the United States, more than 21 million have only one parent in the home.

- Approximately half of these families have only one adult in the home.

- More than 10 million parents, the majority being women, have the sole responsibility for their homes and families with no other person there to assist them in the everyday tasks that go into raising children and earning a living.

Some single mothers are single by choice, others by necessity. Some have left abusive or unacceptable partnerships. Some have been abandoned or widowed. Some are separated from partners for a period of time, others permanently. Some have decided not to marry the father of their child. Many more couples are opting not to marry; however, if their relationship remains stable for two or more years, they are considered to be in a common-law marital situation and are not included in the statistics quoted in this chapter.

- Most of the figures quoted here come from the 1996 census, but updated information gathered by "Child Stats 1999" shows little change from those percentages.

- Unmarried mothers account for about one-third of the annual births in the U.S., although the number of teen moms dropped significantly in the final years of the 20th century.

- Marriage has become less of a "must" in North America during past decades. It is surprising to many people to discover that while about 30 percent of homes have only one parent, only 25 percent have two parents who are married.

- Of these 30-percent single-parent families, 84 percent are children with single mothers and only 16 percent are children with single fathers. This seems pretty uneven, but it is interesting to note that while the number of single-mom homes has stayed roughly the same since the 1996 census figures came out, the number of single-dad homes has doubled to reach the 16-percent figure. Men are more likely to get at least partial custody nowadays, and this is a trend that is growing.

- There are two main differences between single-mom households and those headed by single dads. Many more — about 40 percent — of single mothers have never married. Only one-third of single fathers have never married. The other difference is in the huge disparity in income.

Financial Facts

- Thirty percent of single-parent families live below the $13,000 per year poverty line.

- Sixteen percent of two-parent families are living below the poverty line.

- In 1998, 2.1 million families headed by a single father and 9.8 million families headed by a single mother lived below the poverty line.

- Single-father incomes are about twice as high as single-mother incomes where there is an order in place for family-support payments that either are or are not being made.

- In families where there has been no request for support, the father's income is about three times that of the average single-mother's income.

- Most single moms who do not get support do not get it because the father has insufficient income or has always been entirely absent.

- Most single fathers who do not get support have a much higher income than their ex-wives, or do not seek support from them for other reasons.

- Not receiving child-support payments is one of the major ongoing problems facing single mothers.

- About three-fourths of child-support payments are made. Reporting policies for new hires have improved the collectability of child support by making it harder for delinquent parents to move around to avoid paying. Some states are starting to collect support for grandchildren by garnishing earnings from grandparents where liable parents are under age.

- Of all families below the poverty line, more than one-third are led by women and only one-eighth by single men.

- Child-support amounts run between $2,000 and $3,000 a year on average, about 17 percent of a mother's income and about 7 percent of a father's.

- Fifty-eight percent of custodial parents are awarded child support. More than 30 percent do not want it or choose not to ask for it. For the rest, there is no money available from the absent parent.

Buy any 3, get 1 FREE!

Get a 60-Minute Training Series™ Handbook FREE ($14.95 value)* when you buy any three. See back of order form for full selection of titles.

These are helpful how-to books for you, your employees and co-workers. Add to your library. Use for new-employee training, brown-bag seminars, promotion gifts and more. Choose from many popular titles on a variety of lifestyle, communication, productivity and leadership topics. Exclusively from National Press Publications.

DESKTOP HANDBOOK ORDER FORM

Ordering is easy:

1. Complete both sides of this Order Form, detach, and mail, fax or phone your order to:

    Mail: National Press Publications
    P.O. Box 419107
    Kansas City, MO 64141-6107

    Fax: 1-913-432-0824
    Phone: 1-800-258-7248
    Internet: www.natsem.com

2. Please print:

    Name_____ Position/Title _____

    Company/Organization_____

    Address_____City _____

    State/Province_____ZIP/Postal Code _____

    Telephone (____)_____ Fax (____) _____

    Your e-mail: _____

3. Easy payment:

    ❑ Enclosed is my check or money order for $_____ (total from back).
    Please make payable to National Press Publications.

    Please charge to:
    ❑ MasterCard ❑ VISA ❑ American Express

    Credit Card No. _____ Exp. Date_____

    Signature_____

● ●

MORE WAYS TO SAVE:

SAVE 33%!!! BUY 20-50 COPIES of any title ... pay just $9.95 each ($11.25 Canadian).

SAVE 40%!!! BUY 51 COPIES OR MORE of any title ... pay just $8.95 each ($10.25 Canadian).

* $20.00 in Canada

Buy 3, get 1 FREE!
60-MINUTE TRAINING SERIES™ HANDBOOKS

TITLE	RETAIL PRICE	QTY	TOTAL
8 Steps for Highly Effective Negotiations #424	$14.95		
Assertiveness #4422	$14.95		
Balancing Career and Family #4152	$14.95		
Common Ground #4122	$14.95		
Delegate for Results #4592	$14.95		
The Essentials of Business Writing #4310	$14.95		
Everyday Parenting Solutions #4862	$14.95		
Exceptional Customer Service #4882	$14.95		
Fear & Anger: Slay the Dragons … #4302	$14.95		
Fundamentals of Planning #4301	$14.95		
Getting Things Done #4112	$14.95		
How to Coach an Effective Team #4308	$14.95		
How to De-Junk Your Life #4306	$14.95		
How to Handle Conflict and Confrontation #4952	$14.95		
How to Manage Your Boss #493	$14.95		
How to Supervise People #4102	$14.95		
How to Work With People #4032	$14.95		
Inspire & Motivate: Performance Reviews #4232	$14.95		
Listen Up: Hear What's Really Being Said #4172	$14.95		
Motivation and Goal-Setting #4962	$14.95		
A New Attitude #4432	$14.95		
The New Dynamic Comm. Skills for Women #4309	$14.95		
The Polished Professional #4262	$14.95		
The Power of Innovative Thinking #428	$14.95		
The Power of Self-Managed Teams #4222	$14.95		
Powerful Communication Skills #4132	$14.95		
Present With Confidence #4612	$14.95		
The Secret to Developing Peak Performers #4692	$14.95		
Self-Esteem: The Power to Be Your Best #4642	$14.95		
Shortcuts to Organized Files & Records #4307	$14.95		
The Stress Management Handbook #4842	$14.95		
Supreme Teams: How to Make Teams Work #4303	$14.95		
Thriving on Change #4212	$14.95		
Women and Leadership #4632	$14.95		

Sales Tax		
All purchases subject to state and local sales tax. Questions? Call **1-800-258-7248**	**Subtotal**	$
	Add 7% Sales Tax *(Or add appropriate state and local tax)*	$
	Shipping and Handling *($3 one item; 50¢ each additional item)*	$
	TOTAL	$